FIGHT OR FLIGHT

JOAQUÍN   ZIHUATANEJO

The CoolSpeak Publishing Company

Acknowledgements: "Fight or Flight" was first published in Prairie Schooner. "Archetypes" and "We Are Because They Were" were first published in ¡Manteca!: An Anthology of Afro Latin@ Poets. I am entirely grateful to Natalie Diaz for her brilliance and insights in writing the poem "Fight or Flight" and to Jonathan GNO White for his soul and guidance in writing the poem "Crossfire."

The following is a work of fiction. Names, characters, incidents, business, organizations, and locations are the product of the author's imagination or are used fictitiously. Any resemblance to any actual person alive or dead, events, or locals is entirely coincidental.

Book design by Joaquín Zihuatanejo, Carlos Ojeda Jr. and CoolSpeak Publishing Company.

Cover design by Joaquín Zihuatanejo and Carlos Ojeda Jr.

ISBN- 978-0692424483

Also by Joaquín Zihuatanejo

Books

Family Tree
of fire and rain
    a collaboration with
    natasha carrizosa

Barrio Songs
Like & Share

Audio CDs

Barrio Songs

Stand Up and Be
Heard

Live at Longwood

Child of the Hood
Days

of fire and rain
    a spoken word
    collaboration with
    natasha carrizosa

HOPE 5 MILES

Like & Share

Family Tree

Fight or Flight

Barbaric Yawps
    Best of Joaquín
    Zihuatanejo for
    Students

Order all Joaquín Zihuatanejo books and CDs at
www.jzthepoet.com

Order the EBook version of Like & Share, Family Tree,
Barrio Songs, and OF FIRE AND RAIN at Online
bookstores everywhere.

"The fight is won or lost far away from witnesses — behind the lines, in the gym, and out there on the road, long before I dance under those lights."

-Muhammad Ali

FIGHT

JOAQUÍN ZIHUATANEJO

POEMS

Contents

8

for Aída

Remember when I told you,
you were the kind of woman
I could easily fall in love with?
I did,
I am.

FIGHT OR FLIGHT

*for Dallas Mavericks legend, Eduardo Nájera, the greatest
Mexican basketball player the world would ever know, number
14 & Jesús Santos, the greatest Mexican streetball player the
world would never know, age 14*

1. Fight

Basketball was a game of death to the Aztecs.
They played it like warriors,
till it hurt.
The closest thing they had to a basketball legend
was an angry God named Huitzilopochtli.
None of the Aztec children wanted to be Huitzilopochtli or
Tlaloc.
They all wanted to be their fathers,
who lived and told stories of blood, sweat, and sacrifice
Each of their fathers after the fight,
held the decapitated head of their opponents
in their hands.
Maybe every story comes down to fight or flight.
But oh,
each Aztec child did not know that his father
cried himself to sleep at night,
partly for the lives he had taken
partly for his own which was not.

2. Flight

Basketball was a game of life to the mocosos of my youth.
We played it like Aztecs,
in the dirt.
The closest thing barrio eastside had to a basketball legend
was an angry German named Dirk.
None the mocosos wanted to be Dirk or Kidd.
We all wanted to be Eduardo Nájera,
Who lived through what we lived through, a youth of blood,
sweat, and
sacrifice
Each of their stories ended with Nájera growing wings
pulling the ball
from the sky.

Maybe every story comes down to fight or flight.
But oh,
the mocosos did not know how Nájera
cried the night the Mavericks won their championship,
partly for the shots he had taken
mostly for the ones he had not.

WE ARE BECAUSE THEY WERE

We are Mexican
Because our grandmothers were Mexican
We are American
Because our grandmothers were American
Sometimes we are both at the same time
At Applebee's, Target, and Six Flags Amusement Park
We are both
(Two of the six flags that flew over Texas were
The United States of America and Mexico)
But other times we are not
At border crossings,
In small Texas towns,
In airport security lines
We are only one

We are poets
Because our grandmothers were poets
We are warriors
Because our grandmothers were warriors
In my dream
My grandmother picks cotton
With my grandfather
And their four sons
I cannot tell if it is Southern Oklahoma
Or East Texas in the dream
Though I know they picked cotton in both
Because I was there when they did
Trying my best to help
And though my fingers were small enough
To do the job effectively
I lacked the dexterity and attention span
To be much help at all
I remember watching my grandmother pick cotton
Surrounded on all sides by men
She was so much faster than the others
The ball of cotton
Housed in a crown made of sharp prongs
One thoughtless move
Meant unforgiving cuts

If you ask me today
What is the color most associated with sacrifice
I will tell you
Blood red on a field of stark white

We are comedians
Because our grandmothers were filled with laughter
We are magicians
Because our grandmothers were filled with magic
My grandmother's wand was a rolling pin
My grandmother's cape was an apron
My grandmother had magic in her hands
Her tortillas tasted like revolution
Her frijoles tasted like resistance
Her picadillo tasted like redemption
If the foreigners in the surrounding suburbs
Had ever tasted her lengua
A war would have surely ensued
In those same suburbs today
You will find organic grocery stores
That look sterile and cold
Like hospital floors
In the market deli in the back
They sell seven different kinds of wraps
If she were alive today
My grandmother would laugh loudly and say
"A wrap ain't nothing but a cole' ass taco."

WE WRITE THE WRONGS

"Today my life has come to an end."

-@Miut3

María del Rosario Fuentes,
Mexican Freedom Writer

There is a land
Not far from where I live
Where poets, journalists, and truth seekers
Are hunted and killed
For their words
Where the price of voice
Is sometimes death
At the hands of those
Who would hold justice hostage
Like justice is something one can hold
Little do they know
Some things cannot be silenced
They're simply too loud, too bold
So the tighter they clench their fists
The more poems and tweets, prayers and psalms
Slip from their palms
Even in death
Truth resonates
Truth penetrates
Truth moves in waves
From tweet to street
From voice to choice
It does not end
It only begins
Again and again
It will take so much more than a bullet
To silence the truth
Her blood, the proof
Her words, her truth
Will rise like a phoenix
From a Mexican desert—
In the distance gunshots shatter the silence of night
But they cannot destroy all that is right
There is strength in numbers

And we are many
We are the poets and soothsayers
Who write the wrongs of the world
We believe in peace
The possibility of hope
Justice
And truth
We live for these things
We fight for these things
And if need be
We will die for them
With a pen in our hands
And a curse word for the tyrants of the world
In our throats

SOME KIND OF SACRED MATH

What's in the photo
Is a beautiful brown woman
With hair as long and dark as night
She holds a boy
Who is less beautiful
Less brown than she
The woman wears her smile like a crown
All the while the boy frowns
What's not in the photo
Is the boy's father
The boy met the father once long ago
But all he can remember of his father
Is that his eyes are the color of sky
The beautiful woman is young
Only twenty-one
The boy cannot be more than four
There is some kind of sacred math here

$21 - 4 = 17$

One family minus one father equals
Loretta Lynn playing on the juke box
One family minus one father equals
Act one of Hamlet
One family minus one father equals
Poetry
Equals
Poverty
Equals
New family
Equals
Priorities
Equals
Growing pains
Equals
Hunger pains
Equals
Welfare check
Equals
Are we there yet
Equals

Wanna' whole lotta' love
Equals
This is what happens when push comes to shove
Equals
One half cowboy one half Indian
Equals
Here I go again
On my own
Equals
Broken treaty
Equals
Broken home

We interrupt this equation
To bring you the following word problem:

If a man with eyes the color of sky
Leaves a young woman with hair the hue of night
Right after she gives birth to his first son
How many years will it take before she is more old than young
How many tears will it take before she is more bitter than
    beautiful

In high school the frowning boy learned in journalism class
To solve only for what, where, and when

That same year in algebra
He learned to solve for the two unknown values
In any relationship first
Before even beginning to solve the why

So many years and so much math later
A second photo was taken

What's in the photo
Is a not-so-brown man
Who was once a boy
With a frown for the world
He holds in his arms
A beautiful woman
Whose smile is the answer to all life's equations
She doesn't know it yet
But in her grows their first little girl

If the frowning boy
In the first photo
Could ask the smiling man in the second one
What has all this subtraction
And addition taught you?

The man would hold the boy in his arms
And tell him,

The son is greater than the whole of its parts

FOR THE WHITE GIRL NAMED AFTER A SPICE THAT I DATED IN HIGH SCHOOL

I will not tell you if her name was sugar or paprika or cinnamon

I will tell you that sometimes white people
name their children after tastes
that some people find sweet
and others find rancid

I will tell you she was impossibly pretty
tragically pretty
desperately pretty

with hair like red flame
and skin like snow drift

She was a porcelain doll with hairline cracks
far too delicate and fragile to be handled by a careless barrio boy

I will tell you what I learned from her
I learned that far off foreign suburban streets
can be just as unjust
as the unforgiving streets of the barrio
that there are terrors out there
hiding behind those manicured lawns
that every children's story involving wolves
begins with pretty girls from pretty places

I will not tell you if she laughed or cried when I kissed her

Some memories belong only to the poet
not the poem

I will tell you what I should have told her all those years ago

I'm sorry I couldn't see the wolves for the trees
I'm sorry I couldn't hear your pleas
I'm sorry I couldn't save you
You see,
back then

I was impossibly
I was tragically
I was desperately
trying to save me

ARCHETYPES

3

I will tell you three things about my father and one will be a lie:
my father left the year I was born; my father's heart like mine
and yours is made up of four chambers, but only three work
well; my father's left atrium broke the day he walked away from
me.

There were three of us. We all came from different fathers, but
the same mother. We all have different colored eyes but the
same smile.

We're all different but the same. We're all different but the
same. We're all different but the same.

4

I think I have only loved four women well in my life.

At some point you should take all the money in your wallet and
spend it on the women in your life you have loved well. At the
moment, counting the change in my pocket I currently have just
under seven dollars on me. I would buy the first woman a white
peach because she once moaned passionately after biting into
one. I would buy the second one a pack of sugar free gum
because she is diabetic. I would buy the third one a disposable
camera, which seems insignificant, but oh, can you imagine the
possibilities in those 24 exposures? The fourth woman, I would
give this poem, as I would likely be out of money at this point.
This section of this poem says as much about the fourth
woman's love of poetry as it does about my ability to budget
money well.

I'm writing this poem in an airport. My flight lands at 4:00 PM,
and there's a very good chance my phone will be dead by then.
When I land, I don't want to call the four women I've loved
well, I want to call all the women I did not love well and tell
them just how sorry I am.

I'm sorry. I'm sorry. I'm sorry. I'm sorry.

7

My favorite movie growing up as a kid was The Magnificent Seven. A remake of a classic Japanese film, The Seven Samurai. In terms of film, my favorite childhood movie is an American bastard, but it's a good one. So am I. So are my brothers. You could teach a class on archetypal symbolism from just that film alone.

The star of that film, Yule Brenner, died of lung cancer. Just before he died he shot one of the most poignant and powerful public service announcements. That PSA ends with Yule Brenner staring into your soul from inside the black and white television repeating three words, just...don't...smoke. I swear it must have run seven times a day during the prime time of my youth. And though I can't be certain of it, I think those may have been Yule Brenner's last words.

When I was seven I learned that my father smoked non-filtered Camels, so did Yule Brenner. And though I can't be certain of it, I think in the end it will not be my father's metaphorical broken heart nor will it be his actual broken heart that gets the best of him, in the end it will be his lungs. And I, his first-born son, will not be there to hold his hand when he dies. I will not get to hear his last words. I will not get to ask for or accept his forgiveness. In the end there will be only silence.

I forgive you. I forgive you. I forgive you. I forgive you. I forgive you. I forgive you. I forgive you.

I just found out my flight is delayed. It will not land until 7:00 PM. Will the women I have not loved well forgive me for my silence, or for the times I should have been silent but was not? Will they forgive my carelessness with money, or my carelessness with all four chambers of the human heart? Will they forgive me for loving words more than I loved them? Will they forgive me for all the poems I've written about them or all the poems I haven't written about them?

I want to write a collection of 28 poems. Seven poems for each of the four women I have loved well. And though I love them all, I will reserve the use of closed form for only one of them. I will write her seven Shakespearean sonnets. No, I will write her seven villanelles. No, I will write her seven epic poems written in rhyming couplets. No, I will write her seven powerful and poignant PSAs that will all end the same, with three words.

I love you. I love you. I love you. I love you. I love you. I love you. I love you.

IT'S HARD TO SAY

My flight attendant's name is Moises
A name which has Moses inside of it

What if Moses is inside of my flight attendant
What if he is the shepherd and I the chosen one

I chose the one aisle seat left on the plane
Or rather it chose me, it's hard to say

Moises is a hard name to say
But I like names like his with as many vowels as consonants

Constance is the name of the other flight attendant
A name that despite its meaning has less poetry in it than Moises

Not despite its meaning, but because of it, her name does not fit
She seems the type of woman prone to fits of flight of fancy

If I had to pick three words to describe Moises, one would be
    "fancy"
The other two would be "tall" and "good-looking"

I'm only one of these three things
And now you're wondering which one

A hair under six-one is tall for my mother's people
My father was six-two, my mother was five-one

Constance could have been my father's sister
With their dirty blonde hair and eyes the color of sky

Moises has hair the color of night but eyes more akin to brown
    than black
He could be a brother or at the very least a cousin on my
    mother's side

At the very least I see my father twice a day in the eyes of
    strangers
Despite the fact he left the year I was born

The year I was born my father flew out of my life

I've been trying to write my father's wrongs ever since

Ever since I started writing this poem
Moises has been trying to read it over my shoulder as he
      walks by

My flight attendant's name is Moises
A name which has I and me inside of it

If I read my father this poem, would he smile or would he shush
Would he fold it into a paper plane, would he burn it like a bush

UNDIAGNOSED

for Aiyana

The spray of insulin retracts back into the tip of the needle
Like a star gazer lily shrinking into a seed
The needle is pulled from the skin
An unforgiving anchor breaking the surface of a calm sea
We walk backwards out of the doctor's office
And fall into car seats
Houses, storefronts, restaurants fly by us
Like a reel to reel playing in reverse
Months fly back onto the calendar
As this happens again and again for years
Until she is half the age she is now
That year she will gain 10 pounds within a few months
Stains on her sheets collapse in on themselves
A yellow flower blossoms in reverse
As the smell of urine rises from her mattress
And still time passes
Spring's warmth gives way to winter's chill
Which fades into autumn's gold
Until she sits with me at the dining room table
I am years from old
And she too young to know
How many carbohydrates is in a slice of bread
A glass of milk
A piece of cake
And spaghetti is pronounced pasghetti
It is not something to be avoided or feared
It is messy and delicious
And when she asks me
If we had no forks how would we eat it?
I smile as I grab a handful and shove it in my mouth
She smiles and does the same
A careless game played between child and father
And I realize at this exact moment
That this is not my daughter
And this is not me
This is a poem wrapped in a memory
And just then
I lurch forward
The reel corrects itself

Days, months, years fly by
I grow wrinkles around my eyes
And I realize
I cannot undo what has been done
My way with words
My gift
Is useless
As Diagnosis,
Glucose,
Lantus,
Humalog,
Become part of our everyday vocabulary
I learn her doctors' first names
Which two chairs in the waiting room have rips in the vinyl
And ask her,
Mi'ja, do you need help with your injection
She softly says, no
And the needle penetrates the skin
She winces
Feels the pressure of the spray of insulin
She looks at me and smiles
A small sliver of French bread is 25 carbs
A small bowl of pasta with red sauce is 50
The salad is nominal
The water is zero
The ratio of units of insulin
To carbohydrates is one to seven
First there is autumn
Then there is winter
Then there is spring
First there is math
Then there is needle
Then there is food
In between
Are all those little messes
And careless games
That make this beautiful struggle bearable

NOTHING MORE THAN TREES

The tree that my wife has named Joaquín's tree
leans precariously toward our house.
The young arborist confessed to us before we hired him
that he was not certified,
but he assured us,
"I love nothing more than trees."
When a young man speaks this poetically,
this eloquently about trees,
you hire that young man
to care for your trees.
We did.
Save this one
I said pointing to the leaning tower of bark,
and cut this one down I said pointing to the tree
I felt was encroaching on the one bent by wind and time.
"Cutting this one down is something I cannot do,"
he said with determination in his voice.
He went on to tell me it was a beau-dark.
It was endangered and protected.
We were lucky to have not only one but two in our backyard.
I apologized for even suggesting cutting down something
so rare and special.
He mentioned to me it was unwise to leave the one standing
"that leaned like an old man bending over for his cane."
His words,
not mine.
Without a once a year checkup,
the tree would weaken and likely give way to gravity.
He did not want to ask us to pay him to visit the tree
once a year for a trimming
and to check the foam he had sprayed into three small hollows.
We told him we were happy to incur the cost
to assure the tree would live.
We paid him for his time.
He assured us we would see him this time next year.
So once a year,
for many years to come,
the young man will return to care for my tree.
We will watch my tree grow.
We will watch the young man grow old,
until he gives way to gravity.

and begins to lean himself
When he does
who will return to him
again and again,
who will speak poetically and eloquently about him,
who will say I love nothing more than him?
Who will care for him,
who will save him,
who will prevent him from falling?

THE TRAGEDY OF SUCH JOY

What is to be the children of parents
who fit into each other like puzzle pieces?
Who laugh effortlessly with each other,
who enter a room arm in arm
more one couple than two people.
Where will these children find their poetry?
What wellspring of pain can they pull from?
Will they not write their first poem
until they are well into their thirties
after their second marriage
falls to pieces like dead leaves
in late fall?
But oh, what if they too find their other halves
like their parents before them
early in life?
What if they never know
the sweet beginning
and bitter end of love?
Oh, can you imagine
the tragedy of such joy?

WITH MY VERY OWN EYES

1. A tree split by lightning whose mangled bark and trunk looked like two dragons, each one turning their back on the other
2. A McDonald's cheeseburger framed by two top buns, an occurrence as rare and magical as a Loch Ness Monster or Bigfoot sighting
3. A woman with a bra sized so poorly that she appeared to have four fully functional breasts, each one just as glorious as the other three
4. A blind man walking to his karate class
5. My grandmother Juanita feed a room full of Mexicans with no food whatsoever in the kitchen
6. Sting, yes that Sting, (but is there really any other Sting?) at a record store in Dallas
7. The end of Campbell Road circa 1987, before the construction, before the expansion, before the gentrification, Alphie, Meredith and I stumbled onto it, but it's too sacred to tell you what it was that we saw there
8. A young girl with hair like black flame dance with a giant monarch butterfly beside a river named for the Father, the Son, and the Holy Spirit
9. A small school at the end of a long and winding road on top of a mountain on an island in the middle of the Indian Ocean where children dance and sing and play and learn with a panoramic view of paradise
10. A little big man update his Facebook status on top of a dormant volcano

I will tell you as I told my students, as I tell my daughters, be aware of poems and miracles, they're everywhere, they're all around you, just over the next hill, just around the next corner, waiting for you

FIVE IRREPLACEABLE THINGS LOST IN THE FIRE

The house does not make the list, it has long since been replaced
But the book signed by my favorite author perished

He signed it on the summer solstice
He signed it to me by name

When a writer signs a book to you by name
It says a great deal about his character

Not long ago, a grey bearded character asked me to sign my
    book to him
I smiled and asked, what is your first name?

The kitchen was the first room to burn
Sirens screamed in the night as the flames grew higher

I would gladly have sacrificed every plate, fork, and knife to the
    flames
To save the helpless Tupperware bowl on the countertop I failed
    to refrigerate

There was nothing sacred about the bowl
But the tamale inside was holy, holy, holy

My vinyl copy of The Joshua Tree was sacred, but it burned like
    a ring of fire
I know what you're thinking, surely that album was replaceable

But that particular album's sentimental value
Immensely outweighed it's actual value

Actually that album was given to me
By the girl I lost my virginity to

Now do you see why I lose it every time
I hear the song With or Without You

I have been without that particular album and with that particular
    girl
Since the inferno tried to consume us

33

The flames consumed my mother and me
Or rather a photo of my mother and me

In the photo I am the frowning boy,
Standing in front of the sitting mother

My mother is dark and beautiful and rebellious
She is all the things I want to be

I wanted to save a work of art created by that particular girl
But it burned as the smoke alarm shrieked for us to wake

I awoke too late to save the painting, an abstraction on the
    duality
Of good and evil entitled Heaven and Hell

One half of it was lovely and one half was not
In the end, it turned to ash

But aren't we all like this, one half lovely, one half not
Destined to be ash in the end

AFTER KINNELL, SAINT FRANCIS, AND TWO TEENAGE DAUGHTERS

The teenage girl
Is a thing of wonder
Though she would beg to differ most times
She who feels so uncomfortable in her own skin
She who more times than not
Feels too fat
Too ugly for poetry—
When the world tells our teenage daughters
It is better to be thin and hungry
Than thick and happy
We must either change the world
Or change our daughters—
We must teach them to rejoice in the glory of full-figured flesh
They must learn to worship the gentle curve of hip and thigh
When asked, Marilyn would lie
Size eight she would say
Though she was a twelve
But one cannot truly smile behind a lie
This is why
We hold our daughters tightly
We teach them
True beauty blossoms from within
Only then
Can our daughters begin to see
The loveliness of their blemished skin
The perfection of their imperfect shape
That from the first fourteen years of their lives
To the last fourteen
They have been beautiful all along

THE DIFFERENCE BETWEEN HALF AND WHOLE

I will tell you a story about my sister
You must know that she is not my sister
By blood
But rather my sister by love, by faith, by poetry
Which makes her more my sister
Than my half sister
Who is only my sister by half my blood
Half her blood
My half sister however has no use for my blood
And I, the tragic poet
See my half sister as the manifestation
Of my father's weakness
So she will always be
The archetypal symbol
The reminder that my father
Abandoned his first family
To start a new family
In a far off foreign suburb
In a new house
Filled with new things
And possibly a new kind of love
But this is not my half sister's story
I don't even know what her story would begin to sound like
Nor do I care to know
This is a story of my sister
My sister,
The not so tragic poet,
Is born of Black mother
And brown father
My sister is the love child of Pancho Villa and Billie Holiday
My sister is the love child of Muhammad Ali and Frida Kahlo
My sister floats like a butterfly and stings like a chupacabra
I often wonder does her Black half love her brown half?
Does her brown half and Black half conspire
To beat up the white halves of other mestizos?
She writes about this duality a great deal
I like to think that her Black half writes and her brown half edits
When she performs her poems however
She is some unnamable color between the two
I could read you one of her poems now

But I would rather tell you a story
That took place during the death hour of night
On a stretch of northbound freeway
In Texas
When the car I was driving was filled with only one and a half
living souls
Me, and the Black half of my sister
I don't know where her brown half was that night
Perhaps she left it on the stage
We had just performed poems on
Perhaps it overslept that morning
And she left home without it
But as we drove North
A tragic poet
And one half of a not so tragic poet
For some reason we were both silent
Silent for minutes
Maybe hours
All one and a half of us
In the middle of all that silence
All that nightfall
All that blackness
Maybe it was color of night surrounding us
Like her mother's arms
That prompted her to say it
But if you travel Northbound
On a certain stretch of freeway in Texas
You will come to a sign that reads
"Cotton Gin Road next exit"
And when we came to this sign
That night
My sister
In the middle of all that silence
Shouted a four word poem to the world,
She screamed it
For her mother
For her aunt
For her daughter
And her daughter's someday daughter,
In those four words were revolution
In those four words were redemption
In those four words were all the poems
Her Black half had ever written
And now surely you must wonder

What were the four words
That she screamed into all that darkness?
I will tell you,
When we passed under the sign that read
"Cotton Gin Road next exit"
Looking out the window
The opposite direction of me
My sister said,
"F__k you Eli Whitney"
But the story does not end there
Because as we exited that freeway
And turned onto the road
That led to my house
Just like that,
Her brown half returned,
As she turned to me and asked,
You wanna' stop for some tacos?

CROSSFIRE

for SRV

Sound just ain't the right word
Noise don't do it no justice neither
That symphony that screamed
From them pegs and that bone
And that flat worried note
Best not fall

Sound like
The corner of Marsalis and Ledbetter
Lead Belly Huddie
Huddled between
Big city blues
And dirt road twang
Boy get up

To pluck *dem strangs dat-ah way*
Dig his fingers into that fret board *dat-ah way*
Surely that white boy had Africa in him
They say one drop make you black

They say
To play that old dusty blues
Way he did
You got to be born
The color of struggle
Bet he known hurt and hunger
In a close personal way

Bet he gone to bed hungry
Felt that hunger in every part of himself
Rumbling in the body
The neck
Lingering in his throat
Make him howl at the moon
More wolf than man

Pressin' that wood and electrified wire
Against his palms until fire
Danced from his amplifier

Taking us all higher and higher and higher

Turn good church folk bad
Say it's the best they ever had
South Side blues
Lit by an Oak Cliff fuse
Go on Stevie spank that damn guitar
'Til it get right

He say he stranded
Caught in the crossfire
Sold that soul down at the crossroads
Sound like the corner of Beckley and West Davis
Swear I heard him crying on Zang and Eight
Say he never knew love, so he sang about hate
Hear that wind whispering at Jefferson and Tyler
Believe me Stevie,
Believe you me
When you raised in the Cliffs
You best make sure
You best make sure
You best make sure
You don't fall

BARFLY

He told me he had been an altar boy
as long as he could remember.
But when he turned 18 he took a job
as a bar back
sweeping, mopping, washing glasses, and cleaning the
bathrooms.
One Sunday night
he found a miscarried fetus
(his word for what he saw, fetus)
in a toilet in the women's restroom.
I remember thinking,
how old does a child have to be
before one calls it a baby
and not a fetus?
I simply said,
"My God, what did you do?"
He said, "I'll tell you what I didn't do,
I quit the bar that night
and I never walked into a women's bathroom
or a church again."

OF FATHERS, SONS, AND GHOSTS

Permiso señor, pero ¿puedo hacerte una pregunta?

Excuse me sir, but may I ask you a question?

Though the rest of the conversation happened in Spanish
I will translate for those who do not speak it
For those who have never been lost
Or found
For those who are not fathers
Or sons
For those who have never been both
At the same time
I will try hard not to insert metaphor
Or employ simile
I will strive to avoid hyperbole
But rather tell you as it happened
So let me start at the beginning
The man was a wind blown piñon tree
He was bent at the waist like a question mark
He was beyond old
Ancient may have been a better word
He was Santa Anna
He was Pancho Villa
He was my grandfather's grandfather
He was me 100 years from now
No, one thousand years from now
His hands reached into his pocket
He retrieved his boarding pass
It was as tattered and torn as he was
He handed it to me
His hands were dark and scarred like a landing strip
He asked if he was in the right place
I assured him he was
I told him my flight to San Francisco departed at 11:15
And his flight to Phoenix departed at 1:30
I explained to him that he could simply sit and wait
At the gate
Or go and eat and return
He thanked me
And then proceeded to ask
Every somewhat Latino looking person

If he was in the right place
If he was lost or found
Or somewhere in between
He apologized for his questions
He had so many questions
And he was desperate for someone
Anyone who looked like him
To tell him everything would be okay
But despite all of my answers to all of his questions
He walked through the gate
And accosted more and more people
Some who looked more Latino than I
Others who did not
I wondered if he did so because my Spanish
is not what it should be
(It's true, and I'm ashamed that it's true)
But I listened in as he asked
The third person at our gate
(Who was the most Latino looking
of all the somewhat Latino looking people at our gate)
And though his Spanish was what it should have been
El viejito seguía preguntando mirando Latino persona después de
    mirar Latino persona
Lo siento...
I'm sorry...
The old man kept asking Latino looking person after Latino
looking person
If he was in fact in the right place
So my insecurities about whether or not I looked Latino enough
To be trustworthy were put to rest
He told a small piece of his story to all he spoke with
And I heard most of the conversations
(I choose to believe they were conversations and not secrets)
Writers hear most of the conversations that take place around
    them
Writers cannot be expected to keep secrets
Writers are one half eaves dropper on their fathers' side
One half gossip on their mothers'
(Writers are not easy people to love)
He was on his way to Phoenix to visit his son
Who he had not seen in many years
The son who lived in Phoenix
Was dying
This is tragic of course

But not as tragic as you might think
Remember the old man was a meandering river
He was 2000 years old
So his son could have been an old man as well
But my people have a tendency to toil under the sun
For hours on end
Days on end
Centuries on end
So he may not have been as old as I first thought
So I chose to believe for a moment
That his son was close to my age
And the thought of that made me feel for the father
Made me feel for the son
Made me feel for the ghosts
They were likely to both soon be
And in that instant
I thought of my father
Who I have not spoken to in years
(As much my fault as it is his)
And I realized just then
That my father
May have died without me by his graveside
No last minute flight home to say goodbye
No tears
No remorse
No chance to ask, why
No penance
No absolution
No forgiveness
No resolution
So I stand
And approach the first somewhat fatherless person I see
I pull out a photo of my father and me
And hand it to him
It is as tattered and torn as I am
And I ask him
Is my father a man
Or a ghost
Or the ghost of a man he always was to me
I look around the gate
The terminal
The airport
For anyone who looks somewhat fatherless
And ask them

If I am in the right place
If I am lost or found
Or somewhere in between
I apologize for my questions
I have so many questions
And I am desperate for someone
Anyone who looks like me
To tell me everything will be okay

BEING MISTAKEN FOR SOMETHING WE'RE NOT

"Husband and wife poets, Joaquín Zihuatanejo and Natasha
Carrizosa write poems of love and strife in their collection, Of
Fire and Rain."

The newspaper article read,
"Husband and wife
pen poems of love and strife."
Natasha, my sister, first thought of Charles,
her soon to be husband
would he smile or litigate?
I first thought of my actual wife, Aída,
the only person I've ever known
to beat someone up at a poetry reading
what kind of terror
would she rain down upon me
after reading this hack job of a newspaper article?
But Aída just laughed so hard she farted.
This has been part of our journey,
being mistaken for something we're not.
Two mestizo poets born of east sides and sunflowers,
born of south sides and Egyptian rain.
We both know that half this half that pain
because we lived/live it every day.
She, born of Black mother and brown father
I, born of brown mother and white lies.
This is how it happens or so I've been told
when you're born half and half
it can take a lifetime to feel whole,
but she spoke Spanglish
like mejiafricana for her
like Nuyorican for my wife
like Cornfleics for any kind of cereal.
She reminded me
of the lost boys I used to run with
and her stories sounded like my tíos,
beer in hand, curse word for the world kind of poems,
and I had/have never heard another poet
who sounds so much like me
that we could be confused for husband and wife
when she, who has become my sister, mi 'mana,

in every sense of the word
is the one woman on this whole damn planet
that I hope never to see naked.
She, the strongest limb of my tree
She, unbreakable
She, steady
She, my family

ALL WE NEED

for Aída

The first time my eyes met hers
she wore a dress red as blood.
I thought to myself
there would be something between us.
Since that day
nothing has come between us.
My girl in the red dress
with revolution in her eyes
and fire in her throat
spoke a new language
made up of laughter and sacrifice.
We were so young then,
so lost then.
Some days we still are.
But we have found
in each other
that all we need
is the other.

43

1. That's the age my father left me. He became a ghost, I remained his son.
2.
Three is the most sacred number said the priest, it stands for the Father, the Holy Ghost and the Son. As they all lay there, in a pile at the bottom of some pit, I wonder what was the last thing they imagined or saw before their eyes went dark, was it their fathers, was it some ghost, or was it a stark sky filled with an unforgiving sun?
4.
Chapter 5, Verse 5 of Matthew reads, "Blessed are the meek, for they shall inherit the earth."
6.
Seven is the most sacred number said the teacher because it's the combination of four and three. Four stands for women, three stands for men. Can you imagine what 43 three young men all standing side by side for the same thing looks and feels like? In Mexico sometimes it looks and feels just like death
On December 8, the remains of one of the missing 43 were identified as Alexander Mora. In his family, he is the second youngest of 8.
9.
Ten little Mexican boys standing in a line, ten disappeared and then there were none.
11.
There were 12 disciples, all but one of them would have gladly given their lives for the others. There were 43 students studying to be teachers, all of them would have gladly given their lives for the others.
13.
14.
15.
16.
José Eduardo Bartolo was the youngest. He was 17.
José Ángel Navarrete, was 18, but his friends called him Pepe. His family said he had two passions, soccer and teaching. When asked about his disappearance his father said, ¿por qué es que los generosos, los indefensos, los jóvenes, tienen que pagar por los delitos de adultos?" "why is it that the kind, the defenseless, the young, have to pay for the crimes of adults?"

César Manuel González Hernández was 19. His nickname was "Marilena" because he once "liberated" a delivery van full of the Mexican company's pastries and shared them with his friends and family.

Adan Abraján de la Cruz was 20, his father and his father before him were farmers, but they took pride in knowing that Adan would become a teacher.

Bernardo Flores Alcaraz was 21, his mother held her chest as she told reporters he had a birth mark on his chest that looked like a small kitten's paw.

Cutberto Ortiz Ramos was 22. Miguel Ángel Mendoza Zacarías was 23.

They were friends.

24.

25.

It happened on September 26. It happened on September 26. It happened on September 26.

Miguel Ángel Hernández Martínez was 27, his nickname was Botita, little boot, though there wasn't anything little about him, his friends said he always looked out for anyone smaller than him, which meant almost everyone.

When he was 28 Billy Joel wrote a song called, "Only the Good Die Young."

29.

30.

31.

32.

José Ángel Campos Cantor was the oldest. He was 33 when he died. So was Sam Cooke, so was John Belushi, So was Jesus.

34.

35.

36.

37.

38.

39.

40.

41.

42.

In my culture at the death ceremony we sing a death hymn in Spanish. Can you imagine the sadness of 43 families singing 43 death songs at the same time? Can you imagine the madness of 43 lifeless bodies piled one on top of the other? Were you to stand over that pile, the silence would be deafening.

AN EXCERPT FROM THE GOSPEL ACCORDING TO MY TÍO SILASTINO

"Mi'jo, what you have to understand is that they will always see you as brown and poor first."

"So what do I do tío?"

"Make sure your knife, and your mind, is sharper than theirs."

THE DIFFERENCE
BETWEEN BLACK AND BLUE

I could write a villanelle
to vilify the white overseer
who became beast
when he unleashed
bullets
on an unarmed Black man
Or I could write a haiku on handcuffs
something like:

> They cuff us/they cut
> us/they kill us/they hate us
> there can be no w/e

Or I can write an elegy
for the dead
for the soul
for the bullet hole
for the words left unsaid
Or perhaps an ode for the living
for the weeping
for the mourning
for the healing
Or possibly a pantoum
where the repeating line is:

> Let them kill not one more

Or I could put my pen down
simply close my eyes
and pray
that they
not prey
that this   life
that was taken
be the last one
that this setting son
will rise
that the foolish
will grow wise
we've grown weary

it's true
there's a chalk outline
between Black and blue

THE SHORTEST (AND TRUEST) LOVE STORY EVER WRITTEN

"Love is saving two homemade tortillas for your man…"

(30 minutes later)

"Love is saving one homemade tortilla for your man…"

AN ACTUAL CONVERSATION BETWEEN ME AND AN AWESOME FIFTY SOMETHING YEAR OLD BLACK WOMAN AT MY GARAGE SALE TODAY

Her: (as she held up a pair of floral slim fit jeans) Oh, my niece would love these.

Me: Oh, how nice...

Her: Oh, hell no, she can't fit into these.

Me: Oh, I'm sorry.

Her: She's chunky.

Me: Well, I'm no expert, but I believe thick is in now.

Her: She better hope so.

THE GREATEST OF ALL TIME

Today my personal hero is Muhammad Ali.
You ever notice how he said,
he was the greatest of all time?
Not the greatest boxer of all time.
The greatest of all time.
Greatest leader of all time...Abraham Lincoln?
No. Ali.
Greatest poet of all time...Emily Dickinson?
No. Ali.
For a young Black child
to see this man
on a television screen
in the 60s
stating that he is in fact
the greatest of all time
was an act of truth
and courage
and Light.
My wife's nickname is Ali.
I'm thinking of Muhammad Ali, my wife, and that Black child
as I write this.

EASTER SUNDAY

Today the poem is

an Atheist and a Catholic

respecting each other

despite/because

of this day.

AFTER TEACHING AT A JUVENILE DETENTION CENTER (1)

I am one of those mutable things

that is one thing on one day

and another on the next,

but today

I am merely a teacher

who desperately wants

to save

all of his students,

but I can't.

I can only save myself.

AFTER TEACHING AT A JUVENILE DETENTION CENTER (2)

I have just concluded four weeks of teaching at the Dallas County Juvenile Detention Center. Today was bittersweet and incredibly emotional. There are moments from this experience that I'm certain will turn into short stories and poems. There are moments that I will keep just for me and not share with anyone. But I will share one with you all now. In one of my classes was a quiet Latino student who reminded me of my little brother Mauricio. He was quite possibly the quietest and largest both in height and girth of all the students that I taught. He was a very good student, always writing, always on task, but he never volunteered to share when given the opportunity in class. But on our last day together he volunteered to share a poem with the group. It was so very good, about his Path, the mistakes he had made, and his faith in God to lead him in the right direction. Then at the conclusion of our performance together, an administrator asked the students if they had anything to say to me and the entire group about what this workshop series has meant to them, he raised his hand again to speak. He said, he's never met a good man in his life. He said that I was the first good man that he has ever met, and that I was like a father figure to him. That it took 16 years for him to find someone to look up to, and to work hard not to let down. He went on to say that he never thought much about reading or writing, but now he does. Today I am not a poet or a writer. I will be again tomorrow. But just for right now, just for today...I am a teacher.

THE SMELL OF TORTILLAS AT 30,000 FEET

The young Black woman
sang with her eyes closed.
On a flight when someone
wearing headphones sings
loud enough for you to hear them
it's rude and wrong
in every way possible.
Unless she is young
and Black
and sings Gospel
the way your grandmother made tortillas,
with grace and purpose.
I listened to her sing,
closed my book
and then my eyes,
and I swear
for the briefest of moments
I smelled tortillas
bubbling on a comal
somewhere
in the cabin
of this plane.

"The heights by great mean reached and kept were not attained by sudden flight, but they, while their companions slept, were toiling upward in the night."

-Henry Wadsworth Longfellow

FLIGHT

JOAQUÍN ZIHUATANEJO

SHORT STORIES

Contents

for Rudy

Mi amigo,
Mi maestro,
Thank you for your spirit, and your words,
I carry Anthony and Florence with me, always.

FIGHT OR FLIGHT

The woman in the fifth row looked harmless enough, so opting for the aisle seat in her row was an easy choice. She may have been 70 years old or 90 years old, it was hard to tell. She was so frail and thin, but she had the look of a woman who many years ago was without question the most beautiful woman in any room that she walked into. Her eyes were still dark blue, so odd because I swore I had read once in an online article that eye pigment lightens with old age. She had the eyes of a pretty bully, lovely but filled with pain. I couldn't get over their hue, so dark and deep that they looked fathomless.

I hoped she hadn't noticed me staring at her eyes, but before I could look away she caught me in her peripheral. "Hello," I said weekly.

"Why hello young man." Such a strange reply I thought, I hadn't felt young in years.

"It's nice you took the aisle seat in my row, you never know who you're going to sit next to on a plane these days. I mean it's only for a few hours but you never know if you're sitting next to someone who cheats in poker, cheats on his taxes, or cheats on his wife. I like the look of you. You have a nice face, and I'm glad you chose the seat that you did."

"To be perfectly honest the seat chose me, this was the last aisle seat on the plane and the only row without someone in the middle seat. This airline is a first come first served, seat yourself kind of airline, and not having anyone in the middle seat is as close as you can get to first class on this flight." I said trying to make as little eye contact as possible.

She laughed, my how she laughed. She could hardly catch her breath, and for a moment I grew worried for her. "Are you okay, can I get you some water or something?"

"Oh, no, I'm just fine, you see it's just that we do have someone in the seat between us. I purchased two tickets for this flight, one for me and one for my Harold."

I looked down and saw a small, simple but tasteful urn buckled into the seat between us. "Oh my goodness, where are my manners, we haven't been properly introduced. My name is Gloria Glezer and this is my husband, Harold, Harold Glezer."

"How do you do Gloria?" And then after a few awkward seconds that stretched out as wide as the wings of this Boeing 737 I stammered, "How...do you do...Harold?"

She laughed again and I could tell from her laugh that it was one of those laughs years ago that intoxicated men, that put a spell on them. It was a Daisy Fay Buchanan kind of laugh that Fitzgerald surely modeled after Zelda's. It was as fragile and pretty and as filled with light as a glass menagerie.

"Now son...I'm sorry I failed to get your name."

"Carlos, my name is Carlos."

"Now I like the sound of that, it's a pleasure to meet you Carlos."

"Likewise."

"Now Carlos, I was laughing because surely you must understand that my Harold is dead, quite so actually, thus he cannot answer your inquiries or exchange pleasantries."

I loved that she used words like *inquiries* and *pleasantries* so casually as though lovely sounding words were as common a thing to her as my armrest. I also loved how the words she used sounded emanating from her mouth. She had an exquisite voice, and for the briefest of moments, despite our age difference, I think I may have been falling in love with her, but perhaps it was the thought of her at 30, or 27, or 41 that I was falling in love with. Yes, I think I had fallen in love with the thought of her.

"Carlos, are you married?"

"Yes. 21 years now."

"Well you don't look old enough to have been married such a long time."

"I got married when I was 21, she was 22.". It was at that moment that I realized I could break my life into two separate but equal parts, the half in which I was married to her and the half in which I was not.

"So tell me about her."

I couldn't tell her about last night, about the fight we had, about the things we had broken with our carelessness. I couldn't tell her that for the last few years we had been working so hard to stay married that it actually felt like work, like a chore. Our marriage had become a time clock. Wake up, punch in. Punch out, go to work. Go home, punch in. Go to bed, punch out.

It wasn't Shakespearean. There was no infidelity, no pending war driving me away from her, no blood feud between two families, no plague on either house for that matter. It was all the little things. It was crying children, late mortgage payments, budgets broken like treaties. It was her job that she loved and my job that I hated. All those small and not so small things that disturb the rhythm of your life like awkward pauses in conversations, could even be found in our bedroom. We still made love two or three times a week. Sometimes it was good, but other times, most times actually, we were just going through the motions. Actors on a stage in a bad play who had forgotten their lines. That's what our lovemaking had become.

"I want to love you, I do, but lately it's just too much damn work." That was the last thing she said before walking out last night. When I woke up this morning to finish packing for my flight I noticed her side of the bed. Barely rumpled in spots, partially tucked in, in other spots. I don't know if she slept at her mother's house or a hotel. Part of me feared that wherever she slept last night she may not have been alone.

"It's kind of hard to talk about. We've been going through a rough patch lately. She walked out on me last night." I couldn't believe that I was opening up with such ease to a complete stranger, but there was something so soothing about her, like I could tell her anything and she wouldn't judge me. She had to have been part bartender on her father's side and part therapist on her mother's. "I don't think our marriage is going to last, I think—"

"Do you love her Carlos?"

"Yes." I said it firmly and without hesitation. A good sign I thought.

"Carlos, do you mind if I tell you a story?"

"No ma'am, not at all."

"Carlos, I'm old, not dead, call me Gloria."

Now it was my laughter filling the cabin of the plane. "Certainly Gloria, I would love to hear a story."

"Harold and I married in 1941. I was only 16 and Harold was two years my senior. We, not unlike the world we inhabited, were young and restless and more than a little reckless. The war called him away from me seven months after the wedding. Or rather five months after we found out about the baby. So while I was alone in the world with a child to care for, he was alone fighting for his child a world away. He lost so many friends over there, so when he decided to reenlist after serving his two years I knew it had more to do with revenge than defense of civil liberties. He was walking across a field of wheat when the news reached him and his platoon that the war had ended. It had been raining for three days straight. It was grey and cold, as it had been for a while. If I was a writer I'd tell you that the sun broke through the clouds at that moment like God's love shining down on all the darkness of the world, but this is not a novel, and I am no bard. So I'll simply tell you as he told it to me, the clouds did not part that day and the sun didn't shine for many years after. Let me tell you one thing I know to be true Carlos, the greatest casualties of war are the soldiers who live only to be weighed down by the memories of those lost in the muck and blood of it all. Which makes it much more tragic that during his second tour, his third year away from me, I had a brief affair with a young man I had met in a small cafe on a rainy day.

Affairs starts so simply, a conversation between two rain soaked people in a cafe only to end in such a complex way. I laid with him three times, never in my home, despite the fact that I was young, alone, and terrified I would not allow for my Harold's side of the bed to smell like anyone but him.

So of course when he returned home from the war, I had two choices, to tell him, or to live with the silence, the sadness, the betrayal of it all. But you see Carlos, secrets can fester into malignant tumors when left unspoken.

He came back to me broken. His eyes never had the same shine that they did before the war. For that alone he deserved the truth.

I told him across the breakfast table. I just said it very matter of factly. Trying to make "I had an affair" sound like "pass the butter please" never works.

He was silent for what may have been several minutes or several years, it's hard to say. "I can explain—" I started to say but he cut me off before I could speak the truth into existence.

"No. You don't get to explain." Silence again. "I will ask you three questions. You will answer each question with one word and no more than that. If you speak more than one word after each question, our marriage is over. I will leave, and I will spend the rest of my life trying to find a way not to forgive you. Do you understand me? This is not one of the three questions, just nod yes or no.

I nodded up and down gesturing that I would honor his wish.

"Do you love him?" More silence.

"No."

"Do you love me?" A room full of silence.

"Yes."

"Did you..." he didn't know what to call it "making love" or something much harsher, so he settled for neither. "Did you...you know...in our bed?"

"No." A canyon full of silence.

We sat there at that breakfast table enveloped in an ocean of silence, well over an hour, me never taking my eyes off his face, him never acknowledging mine. Then after what seemed like a sky full of silence he simply said, "I love you too much not to forgive you." And with those words the only vow I had ever taken in my life, the only vow I had ever broken in my life was restored. Do you understand what I'm trying to tell you Carlos?"

"Yes, I think I do Gloria."

"Good. And Carlos one last thing, before you do anything as careless, anything as drastic, anything as stupid as end a marriage whether it's over one giant mistake or all those little things, do me a favor, sleep on it, at least one night.

Now if you'll excuse me Carlos I'm going to close my eyes and rest a bit before we land. I'm an old woman, and I need to rest." She closed her eyes, her voice beginning to drift off into slumber. "Besides, me and my Harold have a big day ahead of us. There's always so much to do, in this life and the next."

PROCLAMATION

Martin was half white. The half that he hated. So he decided early in life that when confronted by white people who were entirely white unlike himself, who was one half white on his father's side and one half Latino on his mother's, that he would demand that they call him Martín. He would do this for two reasons: one, it made him feel better about himself, maybe even more Latino than the math in his blood demanded. And two, it made them feel uncomfortable. He loved the exchange.

"It's a pleasure to meet you Martin."

"It's pronounced Martín."

"I'm sorry?"

"My name. It's pronounced Martín."

"Oh I'm sorry Mar...teen."

And there it was. It was usually no more than half a second. That awkward moment when they were forced to wrap their white lips around that erect i in the second syllable of his name. He lived for that moment. It was only half a second but he always felt there was so much spoken and unspoken in that half second.

Half a second, just long enough to drop an anchor. Just long enough to visualize exploitation, just long enough for a Spanish blade to fall on a brown neck.

Half a second, Just long enough to imagine redemption. In Martín's mind lives had been taken and revolutions had been conceived in half a second. For him resistance was as sharp as a sword, as sharp as an accent mark.

So is was with great resolve that Martín made the

following proclamation to anyone who would listen when he was a young man at war with the world, at war with himself.

"Mira, there ain't no way on God's green earth I will ever end up with a white girl."

"Yeah, Martín needs a dark brown Latina to weed out some of that white in him." They all laughed, but Martín knew there was some truth in what they spoke, or at least it was the closest thing to truth he had ever felt. The only problem was that Martín had spent the last eight years of his life sitting in classrooms surrounded by the very people he hated. In eighth grade he had been singled out for his ease with numbers, his way with words, and from that point on in his educational career he ended up on a talented and gifted track, eventually an advanced placement track that led him all the way to a small but prestigious liberal arts university in Washington state.

And that's where he met her. He first saw her in the library sitting two tables from where he was doing a poor job of pretending to study. Martín had never seen anyone so beautiful in his life. Her hair was red like a forest fire and her eyes were a translucent green. Martín meant to say something to himself but instead whispered aloud the word, *damn*. It caught her attention and she looked over and smiled at Martín. He looked down quickly and closed his eyes. She laughed. When he opened his eyes slowly, he saw the backs of both hands resting just beneath his face, palms down on the table. And there it was, his skin, that constant reminder that he was neither this nor that. Too light to be brown. Too dark to be white. He was an immigrant in his own skin.

Still lost in thought he was startled when he heard her

voice just above him.

"Hey I'm sorry but I couldn't help notice the book on your table, Tortuga. It's amazing. I think Anaya's one of the most important writers of the last 40 years. I just wish that he wrote more. My name is Sarah, what's yours?"

I love you, he thought to himself. "Martin..." he stammered, "well, some people call me Martín."

"Martín, I like that. So Martín," she said it perfectly, not like someone who had taken Spanish in high school but like someone who truly had an understanding of the language. "May I join you?"

"I'm not so sure about the country but it's a free table." An old joke of his, but he said with a smile so it lacked the sharpness that it usually resonated with and she laughed.

"So have you read Bless Me, Ultima?"

Marry me, he thought to himself. "Read it, I've lived it."

"So are you more Antonio or more Florence?"

Save me, he thought to himself. "Florence, definitely Florence."

"Yeah, I could see that."

They talked like this for another hour, with the ease of old friends, leaning into each other's words and laughing at each other's jokes not to be polite but because they truly found hilarity in them. Sarah was late for class so she quickly wrote down her name and number on a piece of paper and slid it across the table thanking him for the conversation.

Martin, I mean Martín, called her that night apologizing for doing so, letting her know that the right thing to do would be to wait for at least a few days if not a week so as not to look too anxious. But he was. Anxious to talk to her again, anxious to see her again. They met the next day in a coffee shop near campus and talked and laughed again like old friends.

Over the next four weeks they had sat and talked and laughed and occasionally argued in no less than six different coffee shops. They had seen five movies, two independent films, one romantic comedy, an action blockbuster, and a midnight showing of Blazing Saddles. They had eaten Vietnamese, Italian, Indian, and what Martin described as a poor excuse for Mexican food.

It wasn't all gather your rosebuds while you may. They argued passionately a few times over politics, the role of the teacher's union in the struggle against state sponsored tests, and they even managed to get into a heated discussion in a frozen yogurt shop as to whether cats or dogs were the pet by which all other pets should be measured.

After knowing each other for five weeks they made love at her apartment on a couch that was usually quite uncomfortable but at the time felt like the closest thing to heaven either of them had ever felt. It wasn't cinematic. It was brief, a bit clumsy, and entirely wonderful.

They married the following year. Their daughter Mary was born not long after that. They realized that on her teacher's salary and his income as a writer for a local newspaper that with the purchase of a house looming in their future a second child would be an expense they couldn't afford. But life has a way of interrupting and four years later Anthony was born. They took the necessary precautions to ensure that life could knock on their door in the future but never enter.

Sarah, whom Martin fell more and more in love with as the years passed, was named teacher of the year seven times in some thirty two years of teaching. And Marty was eventually named editor. His hours increasing disproportionally with the salary he earned.

Their daughter, Mary, had lived up to her name and she and her husband, Tom, who was a stock broker and a Republican of all things, had four children. They lived in Omaha but still visited twice a year. After college their son, Anthony, had taken a teaching placement in Costa Rica, and what was going to be one year of giving back to the less fortunate turned into a love affair between Anthony and another teacher, Alma, that would last a lifetime.

Eventually something other than life found a way to enter and disrupt their lives. They had all become so busy, Sarah with her teaching and Marty with his writing. So much so that Marty wasn't there when Sarah, three days after their 40th wedding anniversary, felt the sharp pain her arm and fell to the ground minutes later, but not before having the wear withal to dial 911 on her phone. Tough as nails, that's how Marty would describe her in the years that followed.

Marty arrived at the hospital in time to say goodbye to her, a small consolation for an otherwise fractured man. He held her hand and for the briefest of moments she opened her eyes barely conscious, but somehow she still managed a crooked smile. Then she closed her eyes and drifted off into something deeper than sleep.

Marty leaned over her and brushed a strand of hair, still

more red than grey, out of her face and behind her ear. "I have to tell you something Sarah, something I've never told you. I made a promise to myself when I was a young man that I would never end up with a woman who looked like you, who looked like my father, that I would somehow sieve the white blood out of me by marrying a woman who was dark and pure. I hated the white half of myself for so long. I was at war with myself before I met you, but you brought more than love into my life. You brought peace. I don't know what started the war. Does anyone ever know? Maybe it was because I remember going to bed hungry as a child. I've never told anyone that, not even you. And I associated that hunger, that pain with my father who left the year I was born. Maybe that's all war ever comes down to, hunger.

Don't you see Sarah, all those years that I hated myself I realize now, it had more to do with my father than me. And it really had nothing to do with the color of his skin, but rather the choices he made and the choices he didn't make. You have given me so much, this life we have, two wonderful children, Mary and Anthony, but more than anything you have given me the ability to forgive. Maybe that's all peace comes down to Sarah, forgiveness and nothing more."

He kissed her hand, her forehead, her lips. She died later that evening. He was holding her hand as it happened. His hand olive in tone laying upon hers so fair and pale. And ever so slowly a broken smile made its way across his face because for the first time in his life he felt at home in his own skin.

KILLING JAY

On his third day of work seven years ago, Javier's commanding officer introduced him to a desk sergeant from the 23rd precinct as Jay. Javier corrected him, "Actually the name's Javier, and it's a family name."

"Calm down Jay, we're your family now." Everyone laughed including Javier but only half-heatedly.

Javier hated the Americanization of his name, and though he put up a fairly good fight the first few days, the name stuck. So before long, the name Jay, went from something he hated to something he tolerated to something he accepted willingly.

Jay loved being a cop, because although his day started and ended at the precinct headquarters just off downtown, his beat covered the White Rock Lake area, Pleasant Grove, and a part of Old East Dallas, which was the barrio of Jay's youth, so Jay got to spend a part of every day at work in the neighborhood that he grew up in. This came in handy for two reasons. One, he knew exactly who to ask in the neighborhood when he needed answers concerning any crime that happened in that part of his beat, the barrio of the Lower East Side. And two, he knew exactly where to stop for lunch to get the best tacos in the entire city, Don Pepe's Taquería, on Henderson Ave.

Jay had come a long way since the days when he would run the streets with the vato locos of the barrio. They never went looking for trouble per say, but rather trouble always seemed to find them.

There were eight of them, and they all lived on Wayne Street. They weren't quite a gang, but they passed for one. They simply called themselves The Wayne Street Eight. There was Gustavo and his little brother Jorge, Mateo and his little brother Jesús. Red was the only white guy in the crew, though he spoke better Spanish than the other seven put together. Jose was the stoic one, and then there was Manny and Javier the two youngest in the bunch.

Manny and Javier were more than friends. In every sense of the word, minus the blood, they were brothers. In fact it was on the steps of La Virgen de Guadalupe Catholic Church that Manny and Javier, using Indian ink and sewing needles heated by a cigarette lighter, gave each other an unassuming tattoo on the back of their hands. A small cross in the wedge of skin between the thumb and pointer finger, their initials visible in two quadrants of the space behind the cross, M/V for Manny, J/R for Javier.

Though they were both the same age, and Manny was a little shorter and smaller than Javier, Manny had been enrolled in the Golden Gloves Youth Boxing League of Dallas as long as anyone could remember. Manny had thrown his first thousand punches before he took his first thousand steps Javier always joked. So between the beatings he would give and take in the ring and the beatings he would only take at home from his stepfather, Manny, despite his small frame, was a boy made of lean muscle and thick skin with two bricks for fists, so whenever anyone tried to start something with Javier, who Manny counted as his family, they had to go through him first. It didn't take long for everyone in the neighborhood to understand that Javier was not to be touched.

It was those days spent running the streets as a kid that gave Javier the street intuition that would serve him on a daily basis as a cop. He always felt he owed a debt of gratitude to all of the gang. He would tell anyone who listened that they would never let him get too deep in the game. He thought maybe they all saw something in him, and that if Javier could make it out of the barrio then he would take the memory of them with him, and they too in turn would be free. The notion was somewhere between poetic and foolish for sure and Jay knew that it was, but he liked thinking it from time to time.

Javier never really had to fight anyone back then, Manny saw to that, and the four oldest in the Eight, had all agreed that one of them, Javier, had too much good in him, so when things got thick or something bordering on violent or criminal was about to go down, Javier was to be left out of it. He remembered a time when they were all talking. Gustavo spoke first, "So tonight were going garage hopping," which is what Gustavo and the others called driving out to the suburbs to look for any house after dark that was owned by someone foolish enough to leave their garage door open. They would bring back bicycles, mopeds, fish tanks, workout equipment, power tools, anything they could pawn. Javier asked them, "Can I go?"

"No, Javier, there's no room for you in the car, just go home and chill." There was always some excuse. After a while Javier stopped asking. He felt hurt and excluded back then, but after many years I think he knew this was an act of love. Big brothers looking out for a littler one, keeping him on the straight and narrow. None of these street kids could ever utter the words, I love you. This is how they showed me, Javier would think to himself when he was no longer a child but rather a man.

Life was often bittersweet for Jay as he rode through the streets of his youth now a man armed to protect those very streets. Today was especially bittersweet for him for two reasons. One, he was breaking in his new partner today, a rookie, just out of the academy named Elizabeth. And second, because today, as it turned out, would be the day that Jay died.

"Hi, my name's Elizabeth Vamos, but everyone calls me Liz." She extended her right hand and to Jay's surprise he found her grip to be quite strong, a little too strong in fact, but Jay let it go. As he figured it must be hard being a woman on the force, so if she hit the weight room twice a day, deepened her voice purposefully a full octave when talking to perps, or shook a man's hand a little firmer and longer than she should, he figured it was her way of letting him know that the field may not be level here, but I'll be damned if you see me as anything but equal. He liked her immediately.

"Jay Rodriguez, it's good to meet you. Actually it's Javier Rodriguez but everyone calls me Jay. So cool to have a fellow Latino for a partner."

"Actually the name's Hungarian."

"Oh, I see...but on the street, I'd let it go if someone assumed you were a Latina. Most of the viejitos, sorry, old folk, won't even speak to you unless you're Mexican American."

"Entendido. Y no te preocupes, sé que viejito significa anciano"

"Damn, are you sure you're not Mexican?"

They both laughed.

Just then the call came in.

Armed robbery at the Mr. M's convenience store on the corner of Willis and Henderson, the two suspects were on foot, one a Caucasian female in her early twenties, the other a Mexican American believed to be in his early forties. They listened as the dispatch officer relayed as much information as she had, he was the one waving the gun around, but they were both believed to be armed and judging from their erratic behavior, both believed to be on a narcotic substance of some kind.

Jay knew the convenience store in question. He had walked into that convenience store hundreds of times as a child and more than a few times as a cop, and on top of that they were merely minutes away. Jay smiled and turned to Liz as he punched the gas. He noticed both her hands, one balled tightly into a fist, the other clenching the armrest so tight her knuckles turned white. So with sirens wailing they pulled into the parking lot. The storeowner pointed across the street to the alley across from them that separated Willis and Monroe. Everyone including Jay knew that gentrification had begun transforming Monroe, Monticello, and all of the streets north of Willis into a collection of remodeled homes that decades ago were dilapidated and worthless but were now filled with IKEA furniture and young, white professionals bordering on affluent. This neighborhood was simply known as The M Streets. The neighborhood south of Willis had yet to be destroyed or rejuvenated, depending on how you look at it, by what both the rich and the poor knew as the cost of progress. Jay knew that the suspects would be south of Willis somewhere not far from where they were in Barrio East Side.

A second cop car pulled up to the scene and Jay instructed them to run point on questioning the store owner and seeing if he had video surveillance footage, which they would find out later he did. A few minutes later Jay and Liz found themselves in the cruiser rolling slowly down the alley adjacent to Willis Avenue. Then they saw them. The two suspects were crouched down between two houses counting slowly and carefully the meager 78 dollars they had made out with. One of the two houses on either side of them looked like it was on the verge of collapse, the other was a simple and modest home that was bordered with a brand new, eight-foot red oak fence.

Liz was the first to exit the cruiser. She immediately yelled, "Police! Freeze!" The older man yelled for the younger girl to run. The young girl fled through the two houses and then south onto Willis Avenue. The older man chose to climb the fence that he had been leaning against to cut through as many yards as possible and perhaps get lost in the mad dash. Jay identified himself and shouted for him to stop but to no avail, so he gave chase and flung himself onto the fence. In the few seconds it took for Jay to climb the fence, the thief had ducked into a shed to hide and noticed a baseball bat leaning in the corner near the garden equipment. He grabbed and held it to his chest breathing slowly though his mouth trying to make as little noise as possible. Jay saw no sign of the suspect in the backyard and immediately noticed the shed. Jay approached it slowly, reached for his communication radio, gave his location, and called for back up. Jay's hand was on his gun but it was not drawn. He placed his hand gently on the shed's door and shouted firmly, "Dallas police! Policia pendejo!" and then after a few agonizing seconds, "Look, I know you're in there...don't make me come in there after you, or we're going to have a misunderstanding!" Then after several antagonizing seconds Jay said, "Look I'm not going to count to three, I'm not going to count to one, come out now slowly with your hands behind your head and your fingers interlaced."

Just then Jay's communication radio sounded, it was Liz stating she had the female suspect in custody a few blocks south of where they left their vehicle. And at that moment the door to the shed exploded. The force of the door opening so abruptly pushed Jay backwards onto his side. The side that had his revolver, so for a second Jay's gun was wedged under the weight of his body and the grass below. And in that second the thief raised the baseball bat above his head and swung it down on Jay, but not before Jay could raise his arm to block the blow. Jay's arm broke instantly under the force of the aluminum bat. He rolled over and reached for his gun with his left hand but the bat came down again, this time on Jay's jaw. He heard a sharp crack and everything began to go blurry. The third and fourth blows were to his ribs, then one blow to his back, the final blow was to his head. Everything went black for a second, then stark white. He was in and out of consciousness, so he remembers what happened next only in pieces.

There were three of them, they were a blur of brown. The oldest looked to be 16, the youngest appeared to be 13. The thief who had the bat raised over his right shoulder never saw them coming, and they tackled him in a fury. The oldest boy grabbed the bat with his left fist and punched at the thief's face repeatedly with the other. The youngest held the thief's knees together forcing the would-be thief to the ground so he couldn't kick, and at that moment the middle one pummeled the thief's chest raining blow after blow down on his chest, neck and face.

In a movie everything happens so slowly, sometimes in slow motion in fact. But in real life it was astonishing to the boys how quick everything happened. Within a few seconds of attacking him, the thief was unconscious and subdued, but the two older boys kept their weight on him for good measure. The youngest crawled over to Jay who was laying motionlessly on the grass of their back yard.

"¿Puedes oírme?" Can you hear me, the boy asked. "Te va a 'ser bien señor." You're gonna' be okay Mister, the boy reassured him. "Como te llamas? Como te llamas?" the boy repeated.

The boy stared into the stunned officer's eyes looking for any signs of life, and just then the boy's round, dark face began to take focus. And in that face were all the faces of his youth. All those lost boys who had saved him so many times. In that face was Manny who he had lost touch with oh so long ago. He realized in that instant that he had been Jay for so long that he had forgotten what it was to be Javier, to be a lost boy with a curse word for the world and nothing to lose. The officer whose breath and voice were muffled by broken ribs, a cracked jaw and a mouth full of blood let out a whispered grunt. It was hard to discern, but it was in Spanish.

"Manny, que soy yo, soy yo...it's me...Javier."

At that moment Javier heard the sounds of approaching sirens and he knew that help was only seconds away.

He woke up later that night in Parkland hospital. The room was filled with flowers and notes of well wishes from fellow officers and friends and family. It was late, and most of his visitors had left choosing to let him rest and recover. He slowly opened his eyes and saw only one face sitting in a chair next to him. It was the face of his young partner, Liz.

"Jay, you're gonna' be okay. The doctors say you'll be able to leave in a few days. I just wanted to let you know that we got them both. The city is talking about giving those three boys who jumped in to help you a medal. They deserve it. Look I know it's hard for you to talk and you're probably tired so I'll let you rest. I'll come by tomorrow and check on you Jay."

Just then he motioned for Liz to come closer, to lean in. He lifted his head off the pillow maybe half an inch in an hapless effort to meet her half way. She noticed and placing her hand behind his head gently forced him to rest as she leaned all the way into him placing her ear close to his lips. And again fighting through injuries and wires that were attempting to lock his jaw in place he whispered for the second time that day, "My name is Javier."

WAR CHILD

I was the only thing my mother and father had in common. My father was a life long military man while my mother played the role of dutiful wife. "Dutiful" that was his word. I'll never forget the time he sat me down on the front porch and said to me, "Antoñio, always remember the best thing a wife can be is dutiful. I'd rather have a wife that's dutiful than beautiful."

The first time he hit her he cried afterwards, curled up in a ball slapping himself on the sides of his head with both open palms. My mother rushed to him, put her arms around him, and consoled him. She…consoled…him.

I don't remember the second time he hit her or the third. After a while I stopped counting. It was usually late at night. That much I remember. I didn't sleep much back then. I still don't. I've had several lovers in my life, I can count them on two hands, I don't know if that makes me the male equivalent of a prude or the male equivalent of a slut. Maybe somewhere between the two, which is where most of us fit I believe. But every lover I've ever had has risen from sleep at some ungodly hour to find me awake reading or writing or watching some rerun of a detective television show that we all know the outcome of but watch it anyway because the sound of that detective's voice reminds us of a favorite uncle, or ex-lover, or an abusive father.

Needless to say like any straight daughter or gay son of an abusive father I found myself attracted to men that reminded me in some strange way of him. Maybe it was the thought that I, unlike my mother could fix a broken man, make him whole again. It's amazing what you can talk yourself into in a crowded bar after a few drinks. That's where I met Ethan. He was beautiful, distant, and brooding so needless to say I found him intoxicating.

We were dating only a few weeks before he grabbed my arm tightly in a dark alley during an argument and told me to shut the hell up.

"Let go of me Ethan...let go of me!"

He did that time.

And so it started, his raised voice. His open palm. His closed fist. Bruises. Time to heal. More bruises. It had been six months.

I sat awake as always last night engulfed by the darkness and silence of it all, when it occurred to me. I had become the one thing in life I swore I would never become. I had become my mother. I began to weep openly. Convulsing at the thought of it, at the thought of my weakness. I woke Ethan. He wasn't happy.

"Damn it Tony you know I have to work in the morning." Rubbing his eyes he continued, "Jesus, what time is it?"

"I don't know." I replied between sobs.

"Why do you always do this. It's always something with you. Why can't you just choose to be happy."

I couldn't tell him it was impossible for me to be happy. I was too filled with hate. I hated the darkness. And the silence. I hated the past and the present and the future, but more than anything I hated his hands which reminded me so much of my father's.

"I was crying tonight because I realize I've fallen in love with an idea, and you've fallen in love with a cliché."

"Just shut up and come back to bed."

"You don't even care that I'm miserable, do you?"

"My God you're such a fag."

"Takes one to blow one."

"What did you say to me?"

"I think you heard me. And if you see a fag, kick his ass."

He rushed me, his face contorted with hate. He grabbed me and threw me against the wall. The sound of glass breaking. I looked up into his eyes, and for a moment I wasn't sure whose eyes were looking back at me, his, some deranged stranger's, or my father's. And before I could block the blow, I felt the bridge of my nose break under the weight of his fist. I crumpled under my own weight like a fallen tree. Crying. And then I felt it. Not pain, but rage.

I sprung up and grabbed him by both shoulders and push him into the door opposite both of us. It opened, revealing the carnage of our relationship to any and all who shared our apartment hallway. I spun him and threw him up and against a wall. As he lifted off his feet I heard the air leave his body. He was stunned, gasping for oxygen that wouldn't come. And before he could regain his breath I punched him in the stomach. Now it was he who collapsed in on himself. I kicked him in the groin, and threw him to the ground. I sat on him pinning his arms under my legs. I punched him again and again. He was screaming, "Stop, please, stop!" but all I could hear was the sound of my own voice shouting.

"You don't have the right to put your hands on me! You can't touch me! You can't hurt me! You can't hit me! You can't hit her! You can't hit her! You can't hit her!" I was still screaming it when my neighbors rushed through the open door and pulled me off of him.

The police were called, so was an ambulance. He didn't press charges. Neither did I.

I heard he spent two days in the hospital before being discharged. I never spoke with him again. A few days later I came home from work to find all of Ethan's things gone. His keys were resting peacefully on the kitchen counter. A small piece of paper was under them, a note, with only one word written on it. "Sorry." I crumpled it up and threw it in the trash.

I looked over by the far wall and there was still broken glass on the floor. I went to the kitchen grabbed a broom and dustpan and began to sweep it up. I realized then it was a picture frame that had fallen. A black and white photo of me and my father sitting on the porch of our home, me a child, he a giant figure looming over me. I looked out a nearby window. The sun was setting over the city, a cool respite after a hot summer's day. I touched the bridge of my nose still swollen and soar. Then I touched the photo with its shattered glass and broken frame. And I realized at that moment that I too had been broken for so long, but for the first time in a long time I felt whole.

A KAHLO-RIVERA KIND OF LOVE

They lived inside a Kahlo-Rivera kind of love.

He was a poet. She was a novelist. They both loved each other but loved words just as much. She wondered if he loved words more than he loved her. He wondered the same.

She published her first novel while teaching high school English to ninth and eleventh grade students. Not pre AP or advanced placement students, she felt that they had already been sold on the power of the well-placed verb. So she turned down her initial offer to teach talented and gifted students at a nearby academy to teach what was called in her district Regular English at an out of the way public high school. She didn't feel there was anything "regular" about her class.

She modeled her child protagonist after a young, female African American student she taught her first year. The student's name was Wylita. The character's name was Toots. It was considered by critics to be one the best coming of age novels for young readers written in the last thirty years. She left her teaching position after only three years when a large press came courting.

He was months into his Doctoral Degree in Creative Writing with a concentration in poetry. It had taken him five years to complete his Masters. He had been published in several anthologies and his university press but had failed to land a book deal. Little did he know that people (in his country anyway) did not buy poetry and that book deal that he yearned for would never come.

She wrote organically, many times choosing to use her first draft over others she had revised, changed, and edited. Words simply came to her. Words had always come to her with such ease. She was a natural storyteller, a gift she had inherited from her grandmother along with blue eyes and dirty blonde hair.

He ached over words, writing slowly, methodically. Pressing the pen down hard when he wrote as if trying to physically intimidate the lines to pour forth. He was the grandson of migrant farm workers. His father moved his mother and his three brothers into the city where he worked for one of the big three on an assembly line. All those years, all those tail lights. That's what his father gave to the world, a long line of red lights stretched out on major freeways as far as the eye could see. He inherited his father's attention to detail and his hair and eyes, both black as a starless night sky.

Success divided them.

She on one side of it.

He on the other.

At first they shared an office, but the sound of her incessant typing drove him away. He blamed it on the noise from the nearby street visible from their office window. But the real reason he hired a contractor to add an addition onto their existing bedroom that would be his office was the fact that he hated the sound of her fingers on the keyboard, all that clicking, a constant reminder of her success and his struggle. She paid for the addition. She paid for most things lately.

He had taken a teaching position as an adjunct professor at a nearby community college but would take the occasional semester off to pursue his muse. He had read at several small literary festivals and had even won a few local poetry slams and placed in the top ten at some larger regional competitions. Unlike many academics he didn't immediately hate poetry slam competitions, but rather grew to hate them as he realized that his poetry didn't resonate with people sitting in a bar on a Friday night after a long day's work who wanted not to be lost in figurative language but rather be carried through a beautiful story that occasionally rhymed.

They sat at the breakfast table as they had hundreds, maybe thousands of times before. He spoke first.

"You have no idea what it's like to be the man behind you."

She looked up from her paper. "What are you talking about?"

"I'm tired of being the man in the corner holding your coat at a book signing."

"Where is this coming from? You're a talented writer—"

"I don't need you to validate my writing."

"What exactly do you need from me then?"

"I need a break. I can't do this anymore."

"Do what?"

"Live in your shadow. It's exhausting."

He looked away. She placed her hand on his, he pulled it away without making eye contact. She knelt before him. Placed her hands on his knees, spread his legs, leaned into him. She placed both hands on the sides of his face and forced him to look into her eyes.

"Listen to me, I love you. I need you to know that."

"I'm leaving you. There's someone else." There wasn't. He was desperate for a way out of that shadow. He was even willing to lie about it.

She backed away. She looked broken like a kite dangling in a tree.

"Who?"

"A student, you don't know her." Words were coming to him easier than they ever had.

"Do you love her?"

"I don't know. I just know that loving you hurts."

They sat there, he in the antique Stickley chair, one of four, that he bought at an estate sale because to him they were lovely despite their feeble state. She on the hard white tiles of the kitchen floor. They sat there comfortably and uncomfortably as the kitchen clock ticked endlessly on an adjacent wall. Then after all those words, after all that silence, she stood, wiped her eyes, and placed the paper under her arm. She walked out of the kitchen but stopped as she crossed the threshold into the dining room and said without turning to look at him.

"I'm going for a run. I do have one more question for you though. If you're here when I get back I'll ask it. If you're not, I won't have to, I'll have my answer."

She never looked back. If she did, she might have seen him sitting there crying. She ran to the lake. It wasn't far. But she sat there for hours looking out on the lake, trying to make sense of it all.

When she returned, the house was empty. She walked into the kitchen, opened the door of the refrigerator, poured herself a glass of water, and that's when she noticed it. The chair he had been sitting in. He had failed to push it in. She placed her hands on its back. She pushed, the chair offered no resistance. And for the first time ever, she looked at the chair, the intricacy of the carving down its legs. Its high back that rose in sharp angles over the shoulders but was never quite stable. The scuffs and scratches that it had collected over all those years. All those imperfections, all those weaknesses. She realized at that moment that some things are beautiful despite their flaws if only for the fact that they endure. While other things that are tarnished and helpless are simply too weak to last.

She pulled out that beautiful, old chair and sat down, and a story came to her.

BROKEN WING

That afternoon my mother was a woman torn in two by concern. Partly for the thought of my newly broken arm and partly for the newly incurred hospital bill I had brought into her life with my carelessness. I too had only two things on my mind: who do I get to sign my cast first, and damn my arm itches.

I knew there was very little I could do about the itching, except maybe bend one of my mother's metal coat hangers into some type of rudimentary scratching device. My mother, however, had the same number of hangers as she did blouses, so I knew she would be beyond mad if one of them came up missing, so I might need to find a wayward twig or borrow a long flat head screw driver from my tío's toolbox to alleviate the itching.

But when it came to who would sign my cast first, there was only one answer: Manny, my best friend. It was he after all who challenged me to jump from the top of my grandfather's truck to the lowest limb of the elm tree that shaded the 1947 Dodge truck, so the gift of the cast was partly due to his dare, partly due to gravity.

That and the fact that Manny would kill me if I let anyone other than my best friend sign my cast first, left me no other choice. And I'm serious about the attempted murder. Even though I had a cast and would not be able to put up much of a fight, he would kick my ass if I let someone put their initials or a smiley face on it before he had a chance to write something like "jump farther next time pendejo" or "try not to think about how bad it itches...hooker!"

When I showed him the cast, Manny said, "Damn it smells!"

"I know, cool, right."

Manny signed his name and underneath wrote, "Sorry you broke your wing Iracus!"

The allusion was misspelled but perfect nonetheless.

THE RINGER

When you are the only Latino sales associate for the third largest litigation service in Dallas, you come to realize a few things. They, and when I say they, I mean white people, will expect you to be stoic, hard working, and above all, a much sought after asset for the company softball team.

"Come on Andy, it's in your blood, you are going to be one of our strongest players for sure! High five bro!" The only thing white people love more than the term "bro," is high fives. Don't they realize they are appropriating both those things, the casual use of the word "bro" and the high five from the very people they enslaved for centuries.

By the way my name is Andres, it took two days for Todd, my boss, to change it to Andrew. A week later Todd walked in and said, "Kick ass tie, Andy...high five!" I've been Andy ever since. Believe me when I say you would hate Todd, not because he's white, but because he's Todd.

So today Todd walks into the break room as I'm eating a kale salad, "Damn Andy, could your lunch be any gayer!" I didn't look up or laugh, my people are stoic, remember.

"Come on Andy, lighten up, I'm just busting your balls. Besides there's someone here I want you to meet. Andy this is Dylan. He's our new 'traveling sales associate.'" He actually used air quotes when he said it. I didn't think anyone used air quotes anymore. I wanted to tell him, "Hey Todd could your air quotes be any gayer?" However the thought of it made my weak gag reflex kick in, and I almost vomited a very tasteless and very expensive lunch all over Todd's oxfords.

I looked up and standing before me was a 6 foot four inch, late twenty something, 220-pound specimen. You could tell by the way his suit was just a little too tight to be comfortable that he was a corn fed, grade-A, college baseball phenom. He was the ringer that Night Flyer Copies had hired under a freelance contract. Oh I'm sorry, I used the word litigation service earlier, but we were a glorified Kinkos that specialized in litigation. If Haynes and Booth needed a deposition copied in triplicate, they brought it to us, not because we were particularly good at what we did, but because we were three floors beneath them in the largest building in downtown Dallas. Don't be impressed by that largest building in downtown Dallas business. They were on floor 3 of 73. We were in the basement level.

Dylan was a blonde haired, blue eyed Christopher Reeve circa 1980. I instantly hated him, not because he was white, but because he was Dylan.

And that's when it hit me, I had failed to mention to Todd or any of my associates for that matter that I had never swung a bat at a baseball, or a softball for that matter, in my entire life. Thinking back on it, the only thing I had ever swung a bat at was a piñata, and most times that papier-mâché burro made me look like an ass swinging at air.

I found myself getting very good at not listening to Todd, so I sorted through the last several conversations between me, Todd and anyone else, to see if I could replicate at the very least Todd's mouth moving as he addressed me, Suzanne, Henry, Jacob, or even the ringer, Dylan, as concerns my abilities on the field...court...no it's field. And that's when I saw it, the image of

Todd's lips mouthing the words in the video recorder of my mind, I could read his lips as if in slow motion as he talked, "Andy...is...a...beast." He went on to tell everyone that between Dylan and Andy, Copy Town USA...horrible name...would not stand a chance against us.

The big game was tomorrow night after work, so I made a point to stop by a sporting good store and ask the first person I found, to sell me a bat for softball, not baseball, just in case there was any difference, turns out there was. I asked for a glove too, they asked for which position? I answered the position that the worst fielder usually plays. They sold me a glove perfectly suited for an outfielder.

That night I googled, "how to swing a bat." I watched several videos before settling on one that was clearer and more thorough than any others. Oddly the video was of a chubby 14-year-old kid from Hackensack, New Jersey. Though he seemed to be a little too pear shaped to be much of an athlete, in the video the kid hit every pitch thrown his way, pitches that were being thrown at great velocity by an older teenager who looked closer to 19. After each swing he would talk about feet placement, shoulder and elbow position, hand-eye coordination. This kid knew his stuff.

I practiced for hours. And after a few hours I have to admit I was amazed by how good I looked in my mirror trying to fake a good swing.

My plan was simple, first I would play right field and pray that a ball not be hit my way. Second I would strike out every time at bat, but damn it, I was determined to look good doing so.

My day at work, which usually felt more like 15 hours than nine, seemed to fly by. Before I knew it I was pulling up to the park, with my orange Night Flyer T-shirt on, number 17 on the back, the name "Andy" silkscreened just above the number. Though Todd insisted that someone with my skills should play a crucial infield position, he finally acquiesced and allowed me to play right field, the position I assured him I was born to play.

When Todd told me I was hitting clean up, I asked Suzanne, "What does that mean?"

"Fourth you retard!" Oh, you would hate Suzanne. Not because she's white, but because…well, you get the picture.

My first bat up I could not believe it, but I actually made contact with the ball on my first swing, and then proceeded to strike out in two quick swings. Though I have to admit, I looked pretty damn good doing it.

The only ball that came my way through the first few innings was a slow grounder that went through Suzanne's legs at first base, I made the scoop, but my throw was several feet off. Dylan, however, was able to adjust and make the catch and dive into third base for the out.

Luckily over the next few innings the only balls to come my way were home runs hit far over the right field fence that were smashed by Copy Town's ringer, a tall guy named Steve. I even cursed and slammed my hand and glove against the fence as though I was generally pissed that I did not get the chance to make a play on them. I was so convincing I had Todd shouting things like, "no worries Andy," or "good hustle Andy!"

The game was tied going into the bottom of the ninth inning. I was so amazed by how well my plan was working. I had even managed to take a walk in the fourth inning and Dylan brought me home for a run. I was so relaxed I even found myself looking past the horror of extra innings to a trip to my natural grocer after this God forsaken game to pick up some squash and peppers to sauté. Copy Town was up to bat. Dylan had been moved to pitcher. Somehow he even managed to make that ridiculous underhand throw look manly. He had struck out the first hitter, but the next two hit singles into the infield, one that Todd mishandled.

I was deep in thought about whether or not I had any extra virgin olive oil, when I heard it. The crack of the bat. I looked up the runners were advancing, everyone was pointing at me and shouting things. It was as if their voices were doing that slow motion, deep voiceover thing that always happens in movies involving sports and a clumsy yet likable hero, you know, "sweep…the…leg," "get…him…a…body…bag." That reminded me I needed to Netflix that remake of The Karate Kid with Jackie Chan. Damn it Andy, I mean Andrew, I mean Andres…focus! I looked up, the ball was heading right for me in what seemed an ever increasing arc. I didn't have time to google fielding. I opened my glove as wide as I could and kept my eye on the ball trying to will it into my glove. My feet shuffled underneath me, the earth shuffled underneath me. I thought I lost the ball for a second in the lights, but just like that, I saw it again. It was descending upon me. This was a big moment for me and worthy of the word "upon."

This moment was not going to end in tragedy. This story was going to be retold year after year at the water cooler as the time the little guy, the good guy came through and saved the day.

I was under it. I was ready to make the catch, ready to be carried off the field, ready to hear the chants of Andy, Andy, Andy! And that's when I heard it. The crack of my nose.

It's funny that I heard it before feeling it; in fact, I don't remember feeling anything. Probably because I was instantly unconscious. I woke up a few minutes later with Todd, Suzanne, and Dylan all standing over me. The blood from my nose had trickled into my mouth and tasted bitter. Suzanne glared at me like I had run over her dog and then backed up to check if it was okay, and in doing so had successfully run over it again. Dylan was laughing his ass off, pointing at me, mimicking blood flowing out of his nose onto his shirt. The entire staff of Copy Town had rushed the field, not to check on me but to lift Helen who had hit the game winning, walk off, in the park home run and carry her off the field. A feat that was not as easy as it sounded as Helen made up in girth what she lacked in height.

Todd just leaned over me, his hands on his knees and said, "Andy, what happened bro?" I had no answer. I just lay there bleeding, and that's when I raised my hand as if to say, "high five dude?" I couldn't believe it, Todd never turned down a high five from anyone. He simply looked at my raised palm, shook his head, turned and walked away.

I was never asked to be a part of the Night Flyer softball team again, and Todd never high fived me again. Thinking back on it now, this wasn't a tragedy after all. As it turns out, in the end I wasn't the clumsy yet likeable hero, but I wasn't Macbeth either. In the end, I was simply me. But I wouldn't go so far as to call it a happy ending. Maybe endings don't have to be happy or sad, maybe they don't have to be tragic or comedic, maybe they can just be endings.

SECOND SIGHT

When Juan was seven years old, he spilled a bowl of cereal on the new carpet in the living room. Juan's mother worked the night shift as a cocktail waitress at the It'll Do Bar. She met Juan's stepfather there. Juan's stepfather, Luís, was a drunk. Not the kind that hugged you too much and told you just how much they loved you man, but the kind that put lit cigarettes out on you. So when Juan spilled that cereal, Luís rose from his recliner, staggered down the hallway toward the coat closet, and returned to the living room with his aluminum baseball bat. Luís turned to face Juan, who was frozen with fear as any seven year old would be. Luís pulled the bat back over his right shoulder, closed his eyes, and swung for the fences. When he opened his eyes, Juan was unconscious on the ground, bleeding from both eyes and his nose.

Luís despite his stupor realized what he had done and fled through the front door into the darkness. When María, Juan's mother, returned home from work hours later it was she who called the ambulance.

The doctor told María that if Juan had immediately been rushed to the hospital the diagnosis might have been different. They might have relieved the pressure to the optic nerve with steroids and orbital decompression, but María who got off work at midnight found her son several hours after the brutal attack, and by then there was nothing anyone could do.

María imagined that Luís returned to Mexico where he had family. She never forgave herself for bringing a monster into her child's life. She never saw Luís again, and after that day Juan never saw anything again.

Traumatic optic neuropathy, that's what the doctor called it, but what all those syllables meant to Juan was that the last thing he would ever see in his life was a man drunk with rage and whiskey swing a baseball bat at his face.

Growing up young and Latino in the barrio of the lower east side is as hard as it sounds, but when you're blind, young, and Latino it goes from being difficult to what Arturo, a neighborhood friend described better than anyone could, "Young, brown, and blind...damn vato...you got triple trouble!"

Juan, who was only seven when he discovered just how dark this world could be, had a saving grace though, actually seven of them, his uncles. When you're a young Latino growing up in the barrio being raised by a single mother your uncles all become a sort of second father to you. Never was this more true than in Juan's case.

When María and Juan returned home from the hospital she called all of her brothers, many of whom still lived in the neighborhood and asked them for two favors concerning Juan. Phone call after phone call through her tears she made each of them promise to help her with Juan knowing that most had children and responsibilities of their own to tend to.

The requests were simple, "Don't ever let him feel sorry for himself. And don't ever let him give up." That was all she asked. Each agreed they would do their best to help in whatever way they could. And though they all lived up to their word, one of Juan's uncles, the only one to never marry and have children of his own, Alejandro, Juan's oldest uncle who Juan affectionately called, Al, took this request to heart the most.

Only two weeks after his return from the hospital, Al stood over Juan's bed at six in the morning.

"Wake up. Juanito...wake up!"

"Tío Al, is that you?"

"Yeah. Okay you know I run every morning, right." Questions asked with declarative sentences, a trait common in all of his uncles.

"Yes, I know," Juan said rolling over and pulling the blanket over his head.

"Well, I'm not feeling like a run today, only a walk, not my usual five miles only a mile or two, and you're gonna' walk it with me."

"Don't be crazy tío, I'll trip and break my neck...I'm going back to sleep."

Tío Al pulled back both covers and a sheet with one sweep of his arm. "I'm sorry mi'jo I'm not asking, I'm telling." He grabbed Juan by the sleeve of the T-shirt he was wearing. It was his favorite T-shirt partly because of the fact that it had a picture of John Travolta dressed in his white suit from Saturday Night Fever on it, one hand on hip, the other pointing to the sky in that famous dance pose of his, and partly because of the fact that it was an old faded iron-on. He could tell by the way it felt rough against his fingers when he touched it, that it was in fact his favorite shirt without asking anyone to prove it so with their sight. All this and the fact that his Abuelita referred to John Travolta as Juan Travoltá made it his go to article of clothing, the T-shirt by which all others would be measured.

Earlier in the year his uncle started reading The Adventures of Huckleberry Finn with him. Juan loved the book because he felt that he and his uncle and Huck were all cut from the same cloth. Like Huck, tío Al was a prankster who loved to laugh. Juan remembered reading a part in which Huck is described as a realist. You know, to Huck, seeing was believing. Sitting up on the edge of his bed, his fingers rubbing against the rough iron-on that had been washed too many times and was beginning to peel off at the corners, Juan realized just then that now to him, feeling was believing.

Begrudgingly he stood up and put on the shorts and socks that his uncle had laid out for him and the tennis shoes that were under his bed.

"How is this going to work? You do know I'm blind, don't you?"

"I'll tell you how it's going to work, with less questions and more listening, so do me a favor, shut up."

"I don't ever remember you being this rude to me when I could see."

"I'm sorry mi'jo, shut up please. Now you are going to grab my right elbow with your left hand, like this." He placed his nephew's hand on his elbow. "We will walk together, you will walk just to the right of me and just behind me. It will be my responsibility to tell you when to step down or step up, slow down or stop. It will be your responsibility to listen and commit some of the things you experience to memory. Trust me, over time you will be able to walk this neighborhood on your own. We will walk every morning and some evenings as well. Some nights I'd like us to walk very late in fact, the way I figure, if you have to do this in darkness, so should I."

The walks were difficult at first. Al was slow and methodical, always pointing out new bushes that were planted, fallen tree limbs, knocked over trash cans, a crack that might trip Juan up, anything that might get in his way for that matter. The first route they walked was down several blocks through the park to his elementary school, and then back. They walked that route for about two months, day and night. Al always challenging Juan to remember sounds associated with certain street corners, placement of trees and play ground equipment, the number of steps that led up to the front door of the barrio elementary school. Juan was a diligent student always listening, always touching, always taking mental notes of things. Then one morning after making it to the front door of the elementary school like they had done countless times before Al sat on the steps with Juan in silence. The sun was rising over the city, the morning air was still cool.

"I'm having problems remembering."

"Remembering what mi'jo?"

"What colors look like. Ask me what black looks like and I can tell you that. But my memory of brown and green and other colors is starting to fade. I don't want to forget." His uncle reached into both his coat pockets pulled out two things, a knife from one, and an orange from the other. He cut the orange down the center and handed half to Juan.

"Mi'jo smell it." Juan held the orange flesh to his nose and inhaled. "That is what the color orange smells like. Put out your hand." Juan held out his hand fingers spread, palm to the sky. Al squeezed his half onto Juan's palm. "That is what the color orange feels like on your skin. Now take a bite from your half." Juan did. "That Juanito is what the color orange tastes like. So tell me about the color orange."

Juan took a second bite before speaking, "It's light. Sticky. Sweet. It's kind of pretty...like a sunrise. Yeah, it's kind of like a sunrise."

"Exactly mi'jo...exactly." Al stood, stretched a bit and turned to look at Juan still sitting there. "Look mi'jo, you know how we've been working with the walking stick lately."

"Yeah, I'm not so good with it."

"You're better than you think." His uncle had even taken to calling Juan, Obi Juan and the walking stick his light saber. "Look, you know the route home better than I do, every turn, every curb, every tree. You're ready, you've been ready for a long time. Here, take this." Al placed the folded up walking stick in his nephew's hands. "I'm heading home. I'll make us some eggs, I'll see you when you get there."

"How am I supposed to do this!"

"If all else fails...use the force Obi Juan."

"What are you talking about tío?" But it was too late, his uncle had already started walking the route back home. Juan could hear his uncle's footsteps, first against the sidewalk and then cutting across the grass. He kept shouting "Tío, don't leave me please, Tío come back!" How hard it must have been to hear those cries and not return to them, but Al ever the faithful uncle kept walking.

Juan began to cry but quickly wiped his tears away as fear gave way to anger. Anger at his uncle quickly turned to anger at his stepfather, which quickly turned to anger at the world, but it was this rage that gave him the resolve to rise. He stood and frantically made his way back up the steps to the front door of the school, a buoy in a sea of darkness.

Juan remembered it was seven strides to the first step down and 18 steps down to the concrete pavilion that was home to the school's flagpole. He recalled that the flagpole was located exactly in the center of the courtyard. He remembered that his uncle laughed once and said, "Man, God must have been feeling very unpatriotic because it looks like one side of this flagpole was struck by lightning. There's a huge dent in it." Actually the dent looked as though it had been made by a baseball bat swung by one of the mocosos of the neighborhood no doubt, but Al wasn't ready to use the noun baseball bat in front of Juan.

Juan remembered what his uncle had said to him, "If you ever get disoriented, remember just make it to the flagpole, feel for the rope ties on both sides. They're about the height of your head. In between the rope ties on one side of the pole is a huge dent, follow the concrete path on the side with the dent toward the sidewalk 27 steps away, then turn right to begin the walk home."

Juan used mental topography retracing his uncle's words, remembering almost perfectly where the steps down and up for the curbs were, always listening intently for traffic coming from any side street. He used the walking stick awkwardly at first but them fell into a rhythm. The incessant tap, tap assuring him that he was walking in just about the center of the sidewalk. Juan couldn't believe it, but he had made it the three blocks down to the park that he and his uncle would cut through. He reached out one arm and walked in the direction he thought was the angle he and his uncle used to enter the park. He was slightly off, so it took him a few minutes to orient himself and find the large wooden sign that welcomed all into the park. It wasn't a large park by any stretch of the imagination, but to a small, blind boy making his way through it for the first time on his own it may have well been a forest.

Juan quickly found the first of the seven trees that he could ricochet off of like a pinball that would lead him almost immediately to the swings. Two sets of four swings. The third swing on the second set was broken, as one hinge had cracked over time. The wooden plank dangled helplessly toward the ground like a bird with a broken wing.

Just past the swings was the monkey bars, and to the right of the monkey bars, the merry-go-round that Juan had actually taken a bad fall off of years ago. He had made it to the two sets of seesaws and walked in between the two as he and his uncle always had. He walked about twenty steps ahead and reached out an arm and felt the metal slide that was always so hot to the touch during those long summer months.

The sound of the end of his walking stick tapping against concrete had returned and he knew he had made it to the basketball court. He found the metal chain link fence that ran the length of the court and opened up at one point to a street, his street. When he reached the corner and felt his stick tap the pole that was home to the street sign that read, Bonita Blvd, he let out a sigh of relief.

Before crossing the street Juan paused for a moment. On the adjacent corner was a taquería. As the bell above the door rang as someone entered the small restaurant, the sound of salsa romántica music inside could be heard. It was quite loud, but beautiful. Something lovely about a broken woman. Juan recognized the voice of the singer, Frankie Ruiz, a favorite of his uncle's. He inhaled deeply and was struck by the smell of tortillas. He could picture them bubbling on the comal, two and three at a time. Just then he heard a young couple step out of the restaurant arguing passionately in Spanish. He smiled, listened intently for the sound of oncoming cars until he knew by the silence there were none in either direction.

Carefully he crossed the street, turned right. Methodically he counted his steps feeling with his shoe the large crack in the sidewalk just in front of Mrs. Roger's house. Until finally he knew he had reached it. He stopped turned to his left and let the tapping of his walking stick guide him up the pebble path that cut through a front yard that was more dirt that grass because of the large live oak tree in the front yard that prevented the sun's light from reaching the remnants of grass below. He climbed the three steps to the concrete porch and stopped to feel the initials he had carved with a twig into the wet cement that his grandfather and uncles poured the year before all of this happened.

He stood, folded up his cane, found the doorknob and turned it. The faint smell of bacon still lingered. He stepped through the living room bumping into an ottoman that had been left directly in the center of the room. "Who left this stupid thing here!" He heard his uncle laughing from the kitchen. Juan bit his lip and made his way into the dining room. He felt the table and found the plate that was placed in front of the chair that had been left slightly pulled out.

"Do you want me to heat up your plate for you mi'jo?"

"No, I'm good." Juan took a bite of cold scrambled eggs and burnt bacon. He sat there eating, thinking about everything. It's hard to say if he knew his uncle was watching him over his shoulder from time to time as he washed dishes. When Juan took the last bite, he pushed the plate away, the sun breaking through the curtains as he did, and ever so slowly like light entering a dark room, a smile crept across his face. Thinking back on it years later, he would count that meal as the best of his life.

JOAQUÍN ZIHUATANEJO

Joaquín Zihuatanejo is a husband, father, teacher, poet, and writer, always in that order. You can support him at www.jzthepoet.com. You can follow him @thepoetjz. You can like him at Joaquin Zihuatanejo. He is the author of five books, Barrio Songs, Of Fire and Rain, Family Tree, Like & Share, and Fight or Flight. He thanks you for believing in his work enough to purchase it. He hopes you find Light in it.

When he was a child, his favorite tío (uncle) leaned over him and asked him, "What do you want to be when you grow up?" "Poet," he replied. He doesn't know where that answer came from, but he knew then and now that he meant it. His tío smiled at him and said "How you gonna' build a house made of poems?" He has never forgotten that conversation with his tío. He and his wife Aída refer to their home as the house made of poems. House Made of Poems is also the title of a forthcoming quasi-autobiographical novel that he is currently writing.

THE END

THE BEGINNING

Now it's time to begin. Now it's your turn, included in this book are 20 lined pages for you to write your poems down. If you find yourself faced with writer's block, remember you have two choices: you can Fight or Flight. I hope you will choose to fight through it and write.

"I got to take what I'm making
and turn it into something,
I got to take what I'm making
and turn it into something
for you.

I got to break what I'm making
and turn it into nothing.
I got to break what I'm making
and turn it into nothing
for you."

-Andy Hull

WRITE

YOU

YOUR POEMS & STORIES

For the students of the Dallas Juvenile Detention Center
who are writing their wrongs.

If you've come this far, I hope you're willing to go a bit farther. Take a photo of one of the poems or stories you've hand written into this book and post it on social media using the following hashtags: #FightorFlight #CoolSpeak.

I'm hoping that students, that people all over the country, all over the world, will come to read each other's poems and stories. Someone once said a poem or story can save a life. Always remember, the life that's saved, may be your own.

CPSIA information can be obtained
at www.ICGtesting.com
Printed in the USA
LVHW081140120922
728117LV00003B/649